HAL•LEONARD

INSTRUMENTAL PLAY-ALONG

AUDIO ACCESS INCLUDED

PLAYBACK+
Speed • Pitch • Balance • Loop

TENOR SAX

Movie and TV Music

Audio Arrangements by Peter Deneff

To access audio visit:
www.halleonard.com/mylibrary

Enter Code
6874-2563-1482-1055

ISBN 978-1-5400-2065-9

HAL•LEONARD®

Visit Hal Leonard Online at
www.halleonard.com

Contact Us:
Hal Leonard
7777 West Bluemound Road
Milwaukee, WI 53213
Email: info@halleonard.com

In Europe contact:
Hal Leonard Europe Limited
Distribution Centre, Newmarket Road
Bury St Edmunds, Suffolk, IP33 3YB
Email: info@halleonardeurope.com

In Australia contact:
Hal Leonard Australia Pty. Ltd.
4 Lentara Court
Cheltenham, Victoria, 3192 Australia
Email: info@halleonard.com.au

THE AVENGERS

from THE AVENGERS

TENOR SAX

Composed by
ALAN SILVESTRI

CAPTAIN AMERICA MARCH

from CAPTAIN AMERICA

TENOR SAX

By ALAN SILVESTRI

DOCTOR WHO XI

TENOR SAX

By MURRAY GOLD

DOWNTON ABBEY
(Theme)

TENOR SAX

Music by JOHN LUNN

GAME OF THRONES

Theme from the HBO Series GAME OF THRONES

TENOR SAX

By RAMIN DJAWADI

GUARDIANS OF THE GALAXY

from GUARDIANS OF THE GALAXY

TENOR SAX

Composed by TYLER BATES,
DIETER HARTMANN, TIMOTHY WILLIAMS
and KURT OLDMAN

HAWAII FIVE-O THEME

from the Television Series

TENOR SAX

By MORT STEVENS

MARRIED LIFE

from UP

TENOR SAX

By MICHAEL GIACCHINO

OUTLANDER THEME
(The Skye Boat Song)

TENOR SAX

Traditional Music
Arranged by BEAR McCREARY

PROLOGUE AND PROLOGUE PART 2

from BEAUTY AND THE BEAST

Tenor Sax

REY'S THEME
from STAR WARS: THE FORCE AWAKENS

TENOR SAX

Music by JOHN WILLIAMS

THEME FROM THE X-FILES

from the Twentieth Century Fox Television Series THE X-FILES

TENOR SAX

By MARK SNOW

TEST DRIVE
from the Motion Picture HOW TO TRAIN YOUR DRAGON

TENOR SAX

By JOHN POWELL